Footprint in the Mud

By Michael Victor Whatley Jr

Dedications

This book is dedicated to.

People in love

Victims of injustice

Lovers of poetry

My family

And my Mother, Diane Reed Whatley, may your soul rest in peace.

FOOTPRINT IN THE MUD

Written & Illustrated By:
Michael Victor Whatley Jr

"I am my worst enemy and greatest Ally because I defeat myself when I quit or don't try."

-Michael Victor Whatley Jr.

Acknowledgments

I would like to 1st acknowledge God. I believe everything happens for a reason, and God gives the hardest battles to his toughest soldiers. Therefore, the things I have been through and endured reflect the strength God has given me.

My Aunts Mary Michelle Seabrooks and Jacquelyn Christian. Thank you for supporting me and helping when I needed it the most.

FOOTPRINT IN THE MUD

© 2024 Michael Victor Whatley Jr.

All rights reserved. No part of this book may be reproduced or transmitted in any form or by any means without written permission from the author.

Table of Contents

Introduction 10
Allusive 14
Power to the People 15
Wake Me Up 17
Protect Your Mind 18
Twist...................................... 19
Incredible 20
Persistence 23
The Streets Keep Calling 25
Pleasant 27
Living Hell 29
Hard to Hide 31
Try 32
Tie My Hands 33
Dream or Nightmare 34
Hidden Enemies 35
Humor 36
Could Have Saved Me 37
Stay Strong 38
Does Money Measure Success ... 39

Her World	41
Mature	42
Another Chance	44
Closed Mouth	45
Glorify	46
Life	47
Love Lost	48
Renewed	49
Hopeless Romantic	51
The Brave	52
Each One	53
Footprint in The Mud	54
Made in Heaven	55
Music	57
What's Up Doc	59
Title Clinched	60
No Problem	62
Never End	63
Draw	64
Prize Fight	66
Make it Right	68
Remind You	69
Senseless	71

Dark Sky	73
Make Way	74
Still Shows	75
Mistress	77
Clearly See	79
Slight Doubt	80
Another Day	81
To Fly	83
Greatest Wealth	84
Crazy in Love	86
Ignorant	87
Real Love	88
Light of God	89
Desolated	91
What is Love	92
Nothing but Love	93
Never Need	94
Sunrise	95
Strength	97
Heavens Knows	98
Teflon	99
Saint at Ease	100
Hopeful	101

Stole My Heart 103
Way Thru Hell 104
The Storm 105
Gun 106
Money 107
Transgress 108
Direction 110
Demonstrate 113
Staying Positive 114
Picking Up the Pieces 115

Introduction

After I released "Trying to Be Grown" Poetry in August 2012, four months later, in December 2012, I began to suffer from Mental Illness and nurtured an attitude that the world owed me something. After a break-in in my apartment, I began to fear for my life and started to hear voices. I wondered what would have happened if I was there. I began to create theories that the police were stealing my book royalties and investigating me for a crime I didn't do. It didn't help when I discovered my book was selling, but I hadn't received any royalties yet.

Back in 2008, when I was 17, I had my first sign of mood-altering symptoms. I was suspended from Hampton University after an altercation with campus security while waiting in the student I.D. line. That was the first time I had been incarcerated, and I participated in Anger Management sessions. I had a problem with authority and eventually learned it was criminal thinking. I grew up in the hood and adopted a criminal mindset. I started shooting dice in elementary and selling drugs at age 14.

After being suspended from Hampton University I ended up getting accepted into Tennessee State University. I wanted to get away from the DMV area, where I had easy access to the streets. I wanted to start fresh, but when they say you can leave the hood, but you can't get the hood out of you, I became an example. I was all the way in Nashville, Tennessee, an 18-year-old teen from Washington, D.C., who didn't know a single person when I arrived, but I had no problem making friends, being that I smoked weed and played sports. Marijuana is definitely a social drug. I connected with a lot of people between 11th grade and college through smoking.

    Once I found out my book had sold, a month later, after seeing the royalties not reflect on my account, I bought the first gun I could get my hands on, and I dropped out of college the first week of February 2013 and returned to D.C. I ended up getting incarcerated for possessing a firearm in D.C. a few weeks after being home. I had a Conditional Status to purchase a pistol in Tennessee. Still, it was illegal to carry guns in D.C. While on pretrial, I ended up violating and being sent to St. Elizabeth Hospital for a mental evaluation. While there, I wrote many of the poems in "Footprint in the Mud." After winning my case in 2014, I continued to struggle with mental health and drug addiction. I was hearing voices, struggled with paranoia grandiose thoughts, and adopted a pessimistic attitude and narcissistic mentality. Even though the drug I was addicted to became legal, it hurt me financially and hindered me from gaining employment. And when the drugs didn't hinder me from employment, my mental health caused me to quit the few jobs I did have.

On December 2nd, 2018, after struggling with Mental Health for six years and smoking marijuana for fourteen years, I had my final meltdown. It was my 5th time being locked up, but this time, I ended up serving four years and seven months incarcerated. During this time away, I wrote more poems sharing my experiences and mind states as I reflected on my life and thoughts. Being imprisoned helped me take time to restore my mental health and rehabilitate from using drugs and alcohol.

The title "Footprint in the Mud" is inspired by my desire to shine a light on injustices and wrongs I have faced that altered my path to success: Having to pay tickets I already paid, as a result having to walk and use public transportation, getting beat down by special police at the hospital while following through for an MRI that they had no record of in their system, having to wait eight months for surgery on my shoulder while suffering tremendous pain, being convicted of a crime in which there was no evidence because the witness got on the stand and committed perjury claiming I did things I didn't do, getting turned down from jobs because of a false conviction as I struggled while living in public housing and living in poverty, being assaulted by authorities and charged with assault after not throwing a single punch or push. Despite all I have been through, I'm able to forgive and move forward. Everything happens for a reason: what doesn't kill you makes you stronger, and you may not get what you want when you want it, but you will receive all you need and deserve with God's grace in God's time.

Allusive

I may be crazy

But far from stupid

The God that made me

Made my dreams lucid

Not much phases me

My fears and tears exclusive

My mom raised me

But the streets made me allusive

Power to the People

>Power to the people
>There is nothing equal
>To the masses on one accord

>Imagine if life was peaceful
>No one beneath you
>But all with something to work towards

>I've been down many times
>But got back up
>The blows I absorbed

>I've played the game time after time
>Missed shots
>But frequently scored

>I've witnessed evolution
>And the revolution

Together, we can't be ignored.

Wake Me Up

Wake me up

It is time to eat

Wake me up

I've had my share of sleep

Wake me up

Thank you, Sun, for rising

Wake me up

Help me expand my horizon

Wake me up

I've had enough rest

Wake me up

For another day on this quest

Protect Your Mind

Someone planted an idea into my mind

It grew and manifest and caused me to be blind

It was like a parasite

It blurred my site

Consumed my thoughts

It tainted my reality

Even the dreams that I sought

It twisted my future

And left a stain in my past

Left a glitch in my perception

Altered my route and path

Twist

If you don't know, you don't know
But ignorance is bliss
If you know, then you know
And you have to resist
The urge, the temptation
The gamble, the risk
In the midst of gentrification
We struggle to exist
Through war we endure
And continue to persist
We march we protest
We throw up our fist
The feeling of pain
Is hard to dismiss
The feeling of love
Is hard not to miss, when gone
So be fond of life's turns and twist

Incredible

MLK gave his I had a dream speech
Which manifested his dream world
Some work hard to buy their dream home
Maybe one day I will find my dream girl

The girl of my dreams
On her finger I will place a ring
She will be my back bone
And topic of songs I sing

Songs and poems about love
Expressing my appreciation for God above
Thankful for the gift of life
For love which has no price

I might drive my dream car
And my drive can make me a star
Reminiscing on my goals and dreams

When they seemed out of reach and far

Closer to my dreams
I can hear freedom ring
Imagining the joy it will bring
Fearless not worried about a thing

If you think your dreams are too extreme
Think of astronauts or deep-sea divers
A new life each dream
A new birth it seems
You shouldn't underestimate survivors

From cavemen to slave men
Hope's of freedom when caged in
Why be afraid when
Death is inevitable

From poor men to paid men
Dirt roads to pavement

The power of dreams and ideas

Incredible

Persistence

Persistence

A lot of resistance to apathy

Can I keep going as if the police were after me

Can I run even when my lungs

Feel like they had enough

Can I keep going

even when the road ahead seems tough

Can I persevere

when I get down, and life gets rough

Can I be clutch in big moments

The stage own it

Fight until the end

No towel being thrown in

I tell myself keep fighting

Even when I get knocked down

Keep writing, reciting

Producing exclusive sounds

Vibes, thrive, dive

Deep into their souls

Traveling this journey and road

As we get old

Often told

You get one life

And don't get younger

Can I keep the hunger

And will to be persistent

Set goals and complete them

For fill my purpose and mission

Persistence

I wont give up but go the distance

The Streets Keep Calling

The streets keep calling

I don't answer but get the messages

I used to be a pessimist

Thinking worst case first pessimistic

But still ended up a statistic

Locked up but still alive

My hopes and dreams seemed unrealistic

Dope boy characteristics

Used to be a mathematician

To the game became conditioned

I might play under conditions

They say everyone has to eat

But it seemed like a competition

instead of a marathon

I was hooked on the marijuana

Recited poems to the streets

Some called me Farrakhan

The streets keep calling

And I don't like its ringtone
Police sirens, firing of the chrome
And Steel; Lie, cheat, steal
No honor amongst thieves
Please believe
We all die but don't get killed
Free will but limited choices
Weigh your options like you weigh the drugs
Listening to the voices over instrumentals
Affects your mental
Some negative some positive
Getting money is the prerogative
In the hood its hard to live
And up to God to give
Chances and opportunities
But life's not fair
So next time the streets call
Tell them I'm not there

Pleasant

I thought I had it all figured out
I thought I knew what life was about
Chasing the ladies, the money, the clout
I was over zealous and had no doubts
I had a plan all the way mapped out
But life is a gamble, and I had crapped out
It still wasn't the end
given a second chance to win
here I am unbroken
back in place after a bend
found my place in the world
now I can smile and grin
knowing that this hell on earth
could feel more like heaven
each breath a blessing
each day a lesson
time which I used to fight is now a friend
future so bright

though some of my past is dem

so dark I can no longer see

only seize the moment

embrace the present

protect my essence

to do things correct is pleasant

Living Hell

I wish I was a child again
I miss my virgin innocence
I wish the suffering could end
If only my life could begin again
I miss my moms nurture
No longer here to correct me
Holding on to the family I have left
Hoping God will protect me
Hoping God will protect us
No longer trying to be grown
And get money in a rush
Just gradually build
Gradually heal
Constant nightmares
Of people mad at me still
Cant please the world
I tried and I failed
Like a modern day slave

Tie My Hands

Threaten my life

Violate my rights

Tie my hands behind my back

But yet I still fight

Rope around my neck tight

Despite being polite

Tie my hands behind my back

But yet I still write

Take away my sight

Block me from the limelight

Tie my hands behind my back

But yet I still shine bright

When what is done in the dark comes to light

They will fear me like dynamite

Tie my hands behind my back

But yet I still will ignite

Dream or Nightmare

Life can be a pleasant dream
Or a terrible nightmare
A dark night where the Moon glares
Or a sunny day bright and clear
A happy movie scene
Or horror film with fright and fear
You can be lonely or have a team
to overcome the things you might bare
It can be foggy, unsure
Or the light can shine green saying go site clear
You can be unarmed, want to scream
Or equipped to fight with the right gear
Like a game with its scheme
Can win or lose no truth or dare
Life can be a pleasant dream
Or a terrible nightmare

Hidden Enemies

No one to beg for mercy
Already cried to God
No one said it would be easy
But I never knew life would be so hard
That they would kick me while I was down
Throw salt on my wounds and scars
That they would lie on me beat me to the ground
Never knew they would take it that far
That they would torture me, throw dirt on my name
Drive me insane until I ended up behind bars
But I wont bend or grieve, hidden enemies
One day time will reveal who you are

Humor

Laugh create a path

For humor

Giggle, wiggle some room

For humor

Have fun, be funny

Be humorous

Be comical, don't let bad times

Dominate you

The past is gone

It isn't a rumor

The future will be here sooner

While you wait

Just don't lose your sense of humor

Could Have Saved Me

You could have saved me
Could have been my Wonder Woman
You could have saved me
Could have been my Cat Woman
You could have saved me
Could have been my Super Woman
You could have saved me
Could have been that Woman
To save me time
Save me from heartache
To save my mind
Save me from heartbreak
If only you were mine
You could have saved me

Stay Strong

Stay strong

Your troubles wont last long

Stay strong

Even though you've been a victim of injustice

and have been wronged

Stay strong

Though your destination and goals

have been prolonged

Stay strong

One day the pain will be gone

Does Money Measure Success

Does money measure success
Controversy at its best
Spilled my heart and made a mess
Love fallen, raised stress
But even in testimony
The money comes after the test
Braveheart, slaved flesh
Measure freedom, more or less
for he with the treasure chest
Blessed with life, cursed with death
Challenged by time
Purchases of time to rest
During a pursuit of happiness
Time flies like a bird who leaves its nest
Caged dreams freedom of press
Lift every voice and sing be my guest
Because every question begins with quest
There is no peace for a piece in a game of chess

Nourishment for nature

Significant others allure
Magnificent the cure

No longer a baby or adolescence
Trying to be grown and insecure

Stronger from life's lessons
I've learned to be mature

Another Chance

A chance to move forward and advance

A chance to look ahead remembering the last glance

A chance to grow and enhance

A chance to stand for something, making a better stance

A chance to love and be loved share romance

A chance to party feel the rhythm and dance

A chance to praise God shout and prance

Grateful and appreciative for another chance

Closed Mouth

They say a closed mouth doesn't get fed
So they tried to make me starve
They say thou who does not work shall not eat
So I just wanted to work hard
They say you slang rock
or have a wicked jump shot
knew the game but couldn't play the part
they say don't talk to cops
even though the blocks hot
I went insane it's like I was too smart
They say the real end up dead or in jail
Kept my lips sealed and just followed my heart
They say that time heals
How would you know how I feel
If I didn't express it through my art

Glorify

I don't glorify the streets
I glorify freedom
I glorify man
Hoping that I can be one
I glorify a father raising his son
Hoping one day I can have me one
I glorify God
Hoping that his will be done

Life

Life is a quest

The only escape from life is death

You have to fight until your last breath

Wrong or right just try your best

Life is a Journey

Get a grip and hold it firmly

Sometimes silence is key

Sometimes speak up like an attorney

Life is a maze

You can go so many ways

You write your story through the days

A living script live plays

Love Lost

I should have told you I love you

I should have put forth the effort to keep you around

I should have kissed you and hugged you

I should have held you down

I should have treated you like a queen

And gave you a crown

I should have never let you go

Now I feel like a clown

I should have kept a smile on your face

And never let you frown

But now the love is lost

Hidden

And cant be found

Renewed

I feel renewed

Thoughts no longer discombobulated

Or misconstrued

My faith stuck

Like its been paste

Super glued

No longer vulnerable

Down and confused

I feel renewed

Brand new though I've been used

I can still shine

Like a pair of polished shoes

I am woke

The saying soaked

If you snooze you lose

Was given a choice

So I chose to choose

To feel renewed

I was playing the field

Or at least worked in it

No time to chill

On the past, no choice but to dwell

Do I have to die to live in heaven

Because my life is a living hell

Hard to Hide

Don't assassinate my character

Don't attack my pride

Don't judge me before you get to know me

Know who I am inside

The cover is just one layer

Give my train of thought a ride

Know my feelings and goals

See my passion will not be denied

Know my dreams and aspirations

All the different ways I tried

To be successful to get ahead

Times I almost died

Lost my sanity caught in vanity

Lost love ones I cried

Lost my freedom, lost rights

The pain is hard to hide

Try

Aim for the stars

If you fall short

You will still fly high

Shoot for the Moon or for Mars

Last resort

You will get bye

Think spaceships over cars

Transport

Thru the sky

Set goals short and far

And never abort

Before you try

Plotted on and captured

For a mate and a check

For a king

It's a constant threat

Checkmate

Debate

Does money measure success

Her World

I need a girl in her own world
Because mine is corrupted
Once she gives me her heart
Hope our love is not ever disrupted
May we be fruitful and multiply
Like God has instructed
And grow old together
Be sure, secure, and trusted

Mature

Take off soar

Even though my hearts sore

Much to live for

Pain but my hearts pure

Have to love like it's a chore

Much to work for

No doubts sure

Confident to the core

Patience is key

One that can open up the door

To the upper room

Where clouds are the floor

Let it rain let it pour

What's Up Doc

What's up doc
Can't you see I'm healthy
Everyone wants to live lavish
Everyone wants to be wealthy
What's up doc
Cant you see I'm content
Though I can't afford to help my mom
pay the rent
What's up doc
I've been reading my Bible
And will do whatever it takes for my survival
What's up doc
I think I just need money
I'm hiding my smile
I know its not funny
What's up doc
Doctor Syed Zaidi
You and I both know
All I need is a lady

Title Clinched

What if I hid my affection for your protection
Would you care anymore or any less then
When its just for your safety
Lately, I feel I've been smothering you
Expressing all my love for you
But what if I hated you
What if I didn't want to make my lady you
Or if you weren't the one I related to
Could you handle it
If I was a dog, and everyday didn't call
Just to show you I mean what I say
Would you still stay
or pay
Me any mind and attention
If I was facing a long time or sentence
And not just my first charge
Because turning away from you would be hard
I already hate to be apart from you

But I will start for you

Or ride the bench

Because your my trophy in the end

So the title is clinched

No Problem

I think about you all day
Though you tell me not to
There are many women in the world
But they have nothing on you
And when I say that
It's from a holistic view
I'm your groupie and fan to
I want to be your man
And mantle
Your man tool
Giving you personal counsel
No games, No console
But if you ask
Its nothing we can't do
And if I'm too much to handle
Just let me know
Because I have no problem
Speeding up
Or taking it slow

I drew a portrait

Of how the world would end

How sometimes all a person really needs

is a friend

Prize Fight

I have no other option but to win
Losing doesn't even cross my mind
I will never look at a clock again
Is what I tell myself sometimes
But now I'm lost in time
Awaiting the biggest match of my life
My freedom and justice on the line
The reigning champion of the world
Enlightenment for the blind
The odds in my favor
And even the evens
God in my favor
And even Allah believers
The uniting of seven heavens
I see the world as one
I look in the mirror
And love what I have become
A young man who understands

The way of the wise

So in the end

When I win

It was never a surprise

Make It Right

Two wrongs don't make it right

But three lefts do

So I haven't been alright

Since I left you

So I left music

And I left clues

About moving forward

And my heart being abused

Thoughts of getting you back

Left me confused

Left me angry with a new attitude

Plus I almost left behind

The dreams I pursued

Two wrongs don't make it right

But three lefts do

So I will take the first step

And the next two

Remind You

I miss you
And wish you the best
It's your last kiss
That relieves my stress
See time is a test
We study each other and pass
You are my favorite subject
And my favorite class
You keep my head on straight
And my mind on task
I never want to slow you down
Or move too fast
Your irreplaceable
And capable
Of doing anything you put your mind to
So even when I lose myself
I know I can always find you
And if you need me

I will be in front

As well as behind you

Because I love you

And I will say it

Just to remind you

Senseless

I used to think

If its not about money

Then it doesn't make sense

Which is senseless

I was now lacking a cent

But not my sense

Trying to avoid a precinct

I sit back and rethink

My money motivated actions

And luxury distractions

That almost caused my ship to sink

Holding on to what's left

Trying to be the captain of my fate

Born of water and spirit

Knowing it's never too late to be great

I cant escape

With my will all alone

There's no I in team

But they depended on me to bring it home

The idea of a new Jerusalem or new Rome

A world where people valued each life

As if it were their own

Dark Sky

Somehow a sunbeam
made it thru a dark sky
Different shades of blue
Cover the nights eye
Pass a group of birds fly
Well flew by
While dying leaves continued to die
Dryer and dry until crumbled
Today I stand humbled
Not trying to be grown but younger
I can't let hard times take me under
So I become the thunder
A roar without the strike
Already hitting my target
Before beginning the fight

Make Way

Sometimes I lay back, try to sleep

and gaze on memories

Thoughts of how things used to be

Then I remember I can't get stuck in the past

Thoughts of how I need to move forward

And which traits I want to carry along to the future

I can't lie there are moments

I miss dearly

As well as moments I don't want back

But they all make me who I am today

A young man still trying to make his way

Still Shows

Radical killings
Mixed feelings
So many want to be the villain
That we are short of heroes

Days dwelling
Evil repelling
Joy stealing
I start back at ground zero

My hearts swelling
Ignorance I'm still baring
Laid back chilling
I'm calm and melo

My minds healing
I see no limits or ceilings
In a city it gets real in

They don't want me with my steel though

I'm still a man

With or without a gun in my hand

Understand

My hearts tucked but love still shows

Mistress

An idol mind in inquiry
Desiring the best
Numerous questions unanswered
Puzzled I'm left
Wondering why
my calls are missed
Still awaiting that first kiss
My mistress
Is just a miss in stress
So all my feelings are dismissed
My lips touched hers before
Only once I do remember
My heart divided in many pieces
My love so sweet and tender
She's busy, me I'm idol
Well at least my mind
Knowing better than to fight
For something that's never been mine

Though I exercised patience

even put in the time

But I know she will always remember

How I was unique and one of a kind

Clearly See

In a lane of my own
I'm unique
On a pedestal
Too high for critiques
Born alone die alone
Yesterday is deceased
So while I'm alive
I manage to rest in peace
Forgiveness in my heart
I have no beef
I reach like a tree to branch
And branch to leaf
My mind expands like Rivers
And Niles to the Sea
After walking endless miles
Finally I can clearly see

Slight Doubt

Her lack of affection now
Makes me wonder
How she really feels about me
I never lied to her
Gave her honesty and ecstasy
Isolated I can't be there for her
But I can't get her out of my mind
I allowed myself to fall
But I never fell behind
I refuse to hold her back
She has class, me nothing but free time
They incarcerated my body
But it only enhanced my free mind
She sounded sad today
I wish I could have eased her pain
I'd hate to see the portrait painted
Without her within the frame

Another Day

Another day to live

Another day to dream

Another day to give

Another day to clean

Give wisdom

Cleanse my soul

Live free with control

Dream deep

Live slow

Steady for the race

Paced for the marathon

Peaceful and calm

With the world in my palms

Another day to see

Another day to hear

See the sun

until it switches places with the Moon

Hear the birds chirp

And sirens thru the noon

Police sirens, fire trucks, and ambulances

An everlasting war

But God gives second chances

To Fly

Sometimes I wish I had wings
To fly like the birds
I looked up at the sky today
And saw a dragon and elephant
Formed by the clouds
I wish I could fly like commercial jets
Or even private
First class sky diving
I believe I can soar
On my feet striving
I wonder what it feels like to fly
And not on a plane
Even time flies as I try to remain sane
To fly versus too fly
An adjective for well dressed
Today I'm ready for the world
Like a birds first time leaving its nest

Greatest Wealth

Today I feel empty
Still as waters with no waves
Chilled with not much to say
My thoughts steady
Focused on how to make my way
My way to success
My way to accomplishment
Without being overburdened
No longer swerving
I've chose my lane
And now its cruise control
I can't lose control
At least of myself
Sun visor down
As I move towards the sun
On a road to riches
My new life has begun
Treasuring my health

And a heap of faith

The greatest wealth

Crazy in Love

Don't hide your love

I know you really care

Off it rubbed

And I will always be there

For you when you need me

Just believe me

Or at least in me

That we will and can be

I hope you understand me

This is real love

The lust just comes in handy

You have a friend in me

Better yet a family away from home

I'm in a zone, a state of insanity

I'm crazy in love

Ignorant

They want me to hide my joy
I feel sorrow yet I smile
Though I may feel sad or lonely
Frowning is not my style
To mask my emotions
To stabilize my mind
I have nothing to work for
Only free time
An outcast forced to fit
A criminal without committing a crime
Happiness just for life
The anger isn't mine
Ignoring the struggle and strife
Plus madness of mankind

Real Love

I thought I met love before
But she makes me reconsider
This time I know it was real
And I want to give her
all the love that I can give her
There is a difference between to love
and to be in love
I want to share my soul with her
And all of the above
She reminds me of an angel
Better yet, a Goddess
I want to share my rib with her
And I'm not just being modest
I want to share my life with her
And anything I have
She means the world to me
More than any gold or cash

Light of God

I am a light of God

They hide like cockroaches when I'm turned on

Surviving off crumbs

Desolated my heart becomes numb

Confused from the iniquity

I can't let them get to me

They talk, I'm more verb

Disturbed

But its nothing I cannot handle

The Lords shield I'm mantled

Beyond mammal

I'm camouflaged with the streets like black top

Ready for the stage, let down the backdrop

Survival and revival of hip hop

Rhythmed poetry

I'm so poetic

No limit no ceilings or attic

So many would like to see me back at it

Never washed up

It seems they just want to watch us

Just follow the light

Desolated

I miss her touch

Pretty eyes and long beautiful hair

I miss her smile, tender love, and care

I met her at church

When she still had virgin ears

A God given bond
I think we make the perfect pair

Mates by soul

Maybe we'll grow old together

She makes me whole

I want it to last forever

Departed before we started

I just want her to stay

Sophisticated and sweet hearted

I just want to make a way

The sound of her voice alone

Is enough to brighten my day

What Is Love

Love is more than a word
Or an expression
Love is everlasting affection
Love is caring
And daring to surpass boundaries
Love is sharing
Creating families
Love is fragile
But not easily broken
Love is a word not easily spoken
God is love
And love is God
It gets you through when times are hard

Nothing but Love

I have nothing but love for you
My brothers and my sisters
No matter your race
Or the color of your skin
I have nothing but love for you
Because it's only one race in the end
I have nothing but love for you
Young teens and adolescence
At that point in your life
Your still learning lessons
I have nothing but love for you
Elders and old folks
Without your blueprint
I would have no hope

Never Need

My memories make moments
Feel like they were yesterday
If only I can relive the past
Some mistakes are permanent
Maybe I was living too fast
People's judgements leave me upset
My sorrow and pain I mask
They ignore their own iniquities
And focus on my flask
Its filled with virtues ingredients
Leading to my discipline and obedience
Things like faith, hope, and diligence
Everlasting replenishment
So I'll never need again

Sunrise

I am the Sun, and she is my Moon
Red, yellow, & purple hills standing between us

I am the one and she is my noon
One hour standing between us

When I rise, she falls
When she rises, I fall, I think they seen us
Following God

We balance each other friends and lovers
I'm always thinking of her

I beam, she glares
Today they are ashamed to stare
Into my face, their eyes squinch
Each day we follow the same sequence
I howl when she is full

A pleasant expression on her face

She knows I am the biggest joker
As well as the spades Ace

Day and night
Each other we chase
Replacing each other's place
With nothing but time to waste

Strength

Stay strong in your convictions

And decisions that make a healthy tomorrow

Success envisioned and followed

Through like days to night

Pride swallowed, yet we still fight

To do the right things

In the midst of animosity and change

And the goals reached for

Become in range and obtained

Therefore, all the work done

Isn't done in vane

Stay Strong

Heaven Knows

Hungry for life
To surpass the strife
Hold my head up high and walk upright
No need to feel ashamed
Point fingers or blame
But the conflict was never light
And my actions were never vane
But high power ordained
See lies change, but truth remains the same
So I'd leave the way I came
And came the way I left
Fighting for life and still escaping death
Ducked off missing, shots fired but never hitting
I'm destined for a prosperous life
I fight blow by blow, I'll go as far as I can go
Not worried because in the end
I know HEAVEN KNOWS

Teflon

Trying to stay focus isn't easy

Getting ready for freedom

Mental and physical freedom

A new start

There is a difference between wise and smart

Wisdom is how you use your smarts

Neglecting your heart

Me I'm so caring

Its hard to take them apart

I'm just a human

Glooming, even when I'm in darkness

They say the first step is the hardest

But that step is already taken

I maneuver through a spiritual awakening

I was sleep and slept on

Now I hold my chest out

Like it is made of Teflon

Saint at Ease

I'm not stressed or worried about a thing

I'm blessed and feeling like a king

I can hear freedoms ring

Please don't judge me by my cover but content

An innocent conscience

Is what I possess

I'm a giver and not a taker

So I'll take what's left

I heard they save the best for last anyway

The greatest gift life

So I appreciate every day

A mind state of devouring any obstacle in my way

I'm unstoppable but not untouchable.

Hated but lovable

Just trying to live comfortable

I'm a saint at ease.

Hopeful

Almost losing myself
I'm close to the edge
Crazy is a mindset of not caring
Which is not so bad
Nor good
I'm not crazy
More misunderstood
Trying my best to be a saint
Drowned by temptations
I'm not culpable
But the penalty I'm facing
Head high I stand
The heart of my nation
Stuck in reality but dream chasing
I had a dream
The famous words of Doctor King
And dreamers worldwide
Today past dreams and reality coincide

Which gives me hope for the future

Hope for peace

Hope for building

Hope for love

Hope for healing

Stole My Heart

I want to put a ring on her finger
Bring her, to family cookouts
She robbed me for my heart
While I was the lookout
She stole it with ease
I gave her the keys to every vault
I admit it's my fault
So only I got caught
Caught with my guard down
My rib has nothing to guard now
But as long as I have her
Life isn't as hard now

Way Thru Hell

I wake up and thank the Lord
For life, for a new day,
And for the breath in my lungs
For the setting of the Moon
And rise of the sun
A man I'm only one, not defined by a gun
From crawling I walk
Stand with no intentions to run
Thy kingdom come, I've came, I've saw
Love and win
Is how I define the law
My mission raw, left undone
A song unsung
For integrity I hold my tongue
Hoping things be done
As it is in heaven
While I make my way through hell

The Storm

The storm is coming

Prediction of rain today

Thunder bolting, let it rain away

Dark clouds, maybe a little sun

Scattered showers

Renewal and cleansing

Heavens cries from above dispensing

The storm is coming

Everyone take cover

Grab your rain coats

And your umbrellas

The Lord roars

While mother nature is soaked

Nourishment to all life

Replenishment of hope

Gun

Give **U**nity **N**o

We murder each other

Get **U**nified **N**o

We have no understanding

Give **U**nity **N**o

I am the keeper of my brother

Get **U**nified **N**o

A genocidal famine

Get **U**p **N**ow

Time waits for no man

Go **U**tilize **N**ow

The revelation of Gods plan

Money

They say money is the root of evil
At least that's what it does to peoples
Thought process, corrupt thinking
Stunting, wanting
The most and never less
A piece of paper encrypted
With numbers and codes
Bronze, silver, gold
Coltan or diamonds
Outshining, seems to never get old
Gold for the function of T.V.'s
Coltan for cell phones
A diamond on ladies' finger
To make sure she comes home
Merchants and merchandising
Trading things you own
But it's a fact you can live on necessities alone

Transgress

Shall my knowledge continue to grow

Like the trunk of a tree

What more do I need to know

Rather I hold my integrity

As my transgressors reveal iniquity

Should I immerse into the sea

With transgressive immunity

Or stay hidden in the shadows

For no one to see

My background and roots so deep

I see the future within my sleep

I awake and try to manifest a destiny of peace

Misunderstood until given the opportunity to speak

Am I weak for turning the cheek

I consider it a strength

Because fighting causes more tension

I reach for prosperity

And my life to be lengthened

To the maximum extension

As a tree in the rainforest

I stand tall and well-nourished

And my words are repeated

Like a classic songs chorus

Direction

Since I lost my mom
I lost a major part of me

I lost part of my heart
And my drive for artistry

My motivation to draw
And write poetry

I found myself depressed
And expressed it openly

When asked how I felt on a scale of 1 to 10
It took a year to pass a 3

Finally reaching a 4
I wish I could hurt no more
But nothing can bring her back

All I have is memories
Of love and care tenderly

Tough love as well
Things got rough we endured hell
When love became an enemy

Hate drowned my energy
Things fall apart
And become hard to reassembly

But passion still lived in me
So, I reached deep inside
And tried, strived to get pass writers block
That which makes a writer stop
Continuance someone sparked
Came to far to give up
Here I am back to art
Knowing where I left off
Finding a place to start

My mother my heart

"Do what you do best"

One of the last things she said to me

Looking down from heaven

Me incarcerated I know is sad to see

But to get a second chance is truly a blessing

Learning my lesson

Fixing my errors

Strengthening my aura

And imperfections

Everything happens for a reason

Now I'm in the right direction

Demonstrate

Let me replace any hate with faith
From any danger feel safe
Make it to first base, then around to home plate
When things slow down
Let me pick up the pace
Let me overcome any adversity I face
Let me appreciate; let me live with grace
Let me forgive myself
And feel like my wrongdoings are erased
Let me replace any doubt with faith
Live life like a marathon and not a race
Let me achieve all the goals I chase
Let me believe life's test I can ace
And whenever I fall short or fail
Let me recuperate
Let me be more than talk
Watch me demonstrate

Staying Positive

Trying to stay positive
Keep my mind out of the gutter
Trying to stay positive
A day I was given another

Have to stay positive
I was given another breath
Have to stay positive
I still haven't reached death

No one wants to, but we all die
Have to stay positive
Keep your head up high

Staying positive means having appreciation
Wanting more
But at the same time being complacent

Picking Up the Pieces

Picking up the pieces
Where should I start
Picking up the pieces
Some rigid some sharp
Picking up the pieces
Puzzling but a work of art
Picking up the pieces
It takes time, and you have to be a little smart
Picking up the pieces
I'll find my mind, I'll find my heart
Picking up the pieces
It's like everything fell apart

www.ingramcontent.com/pod-product-compliance
Lightning Source LLC
LaVergne TN
LVHW052258070426
835507LV00036B/3325